Lunch Box Recipes- 10 recipes and ideas for kids packed lunches

Family Cooking Series

by Debbie Madson

www.kids-cooking-activities.com

© Copyright 2017

All rights Reserved. No part of this publication or the information in it may be quoted from or reproduced in any form by means such as printing, scanning, photocopying or otherwise without prior written permission of the copyright holder.

Disclaimer and Terms of Use: Effort has been made to ensure that the information in this book is accurate and complete, however, the author and the publisher do not warrant the accuracy of the information, text and graphics contained within the book due to the rapidly changing nature of science, research, known and unknown facts and internet. The Author and the publisher do not hold any responsibility for errors, omissions or contrary interpretation of the subject matter herein. This book is presented solely for motivational and informational purposes only.

Table of Contents

INTRODUCTION 8

Tips for Packing Lunches for School 9

Add some Vegetables to Lunch 12

WRAPS AND ROLLS 13

    Turkey Veggie Wrap 14

    Spring Rolls 15

    Chicken Salad Rolls 17

    Taco Salad Wraps 18

    Easy Peasy Lasagna Rolls 19

    Scrambled Egg Burritos 20

    Omelet Burrito 21

    Chicken Wraps 22

    Pizza Scrolls 23

    Ham Salad Wrap 24

    Veggie Roll Me Ups 25

    Ham and Apple Tortilla Wraps 26

DIPS AND DIPPERS 27

    Broccoli Dip 28

    White-Bean Dip 29

    Greek Yogurt Guacamole Dip 30

    Skillet Nacho Dip 31

    Baked Onion Dip 32

    Chicken Fingers with Honey-Mustard Sauce 33

    Edamame Hummus 34

    Veggies and Pizza Dip 35

    Salsa Bean Dip 36

    Black Bean & Tomato Salsa 37

    Feta & Herb Dip 38

    Spinach Veggie Dip 39

    Easy Lunchbox Apples 40

    Creamy Fruit Dip 41

    Cinnamon Yogurt Snack Dip 42

Main Dishes with Veggies 43

    Lunchtime Sloppy Joe 44

    Stir Fry Thermos Lunch 45

    Easy Spaghetti with Sauce 46

    Layered Eggplant Lunch 47

    Chili Mac Supper 48

    Sesame Noodles 49

    Peanut Sauce Spaghetti 50

    Gnocchi with Marinara 51

    Veggie Burgers 52

    Easy Taco Pie 53

    Tortellini with Peas 54

    Corn and Beef Hash 55

    Tuna Vegetable Alfredo 56

    Beans and Rice Thermos Meal 57

Easiest Mac and Cheese 58

SOUPS 59

    Chicken Noodle Soup with Spinach 60

    Quick Microwave Tomato Soup 61

    Italian Pasta Soup 62

    Ham Pea Soup That Kids actually like! 63

    Steak and Onion Soup 64

    Corn, Sausage and Potato Soup 65

    Chicken Chowder 66

    Ham Macaroni and Cheese Chowder 67

    Pepperoni Pizza Soup 68

    Chicken Taco Soup 69

SALADS 70

    Mediterranean Tuna Salad 71

    Tuna Pasta Salad 72

    Pepper Bow Tie Pasta 73

    Colorful Fruit Salad 74

    Easy Chef's Salad 75

    No Cabbage Cole Slaw 76

    Salad Shaker 77

    Fruity Rice Salad 78

    Ramen Turkey Slaw 79

    Smoked Salmon and Pasta in Lemon Cream Sauce 80

    Crunchy Romaine Berry Salad 81

    Greek Salad 82

    Ham and Cheese Tortellini Salad 83

    Middle Eastern Salad 84

    Sweet Lunchbox Noodles.. 85

    Pasta and Broccoli Salad 86

    Salmon Salad.. 87

    Pepperoni Salad 88

    Fruit and Nutty Salmon Salad 89

    Ranch Chicken and Pepper Salad....................................... 90

SANDWICHES 91

    Cold Cut sandwich.. 92

    Italian Au Jus French Sandwich 93

    Biscuit Sticks.. 94

    Pineapple Cream Cheese Sandwich 95

    Pizza Dog Boat Bites.. 96

    Classic Egg Salad... 97

    Pear and Cheese Sandwiches.. 98

    Pizza Quesadillas 99

    Fish Stick Burgers 100

    Chicken Salad Sandwiches 101

    Fruited Bagel Spread 102

    Bacon Double Grilled Cheese... 103

    Make Ahead Subs.. 104

    Turkey Burger Pita Wraps 105

BTST Sandwich 106

Club Salad Pitas 107

More Main Dishes 108

Peanut Satay Chicken Drumsticks...109

Fruity Oatmeal in a Thermos 110

Rice Balls 111

SNACKS & TREATS 112

Pumpkin Seed Trail Mix 113

Frozen Strawbana Smoothies 114

Strawberry Oatmeal Bars..115

Chewy Oatmeal Raisin Cookies..116

Apple-Cinnamon Granola..117

PB Chocolate Rice Krispy Treats..118

Homemade Pecan Sandies..119

Oat Rice PB Balls 120

Grape and Pecans in a Thermos 121

INTRODUCTION

Kids require a wide range of healthy foods to fuel both their body and mind while at school. Although everyone knows that vegetables and fruits are very healthy, it's well known that kids are now eating a lot of processed food.

One of the best ways to reduce junk food is by replacing it with fresh fruits and vegetables and by encouraging kids to be more active. There are many healthy school lunch ideas that you can make for your children with a little planning ahead. Getting your kids involved in the planning, preparing and packing their lunch will put a lot less stress on the parents, as well as get them excited to eat what they've created.

You'll not only contribute to the good health of your kids with these ideas but also save money. Many local stores have great bento boxes as well as other sectioned lunch boxes which make packed lunches more fun.

Go ahead and try out something fun and unique in your kids' lunches, this book has 100 healthy and fun lunch ideas to get your creativity flowing.

Tips for Packing Lunches for School

- The more you get your children involved in the packing of their lunch the more likely they will eat it. Give them choices so that they can feel responsible but make those chooses good ones. One way of doing this is to categorize what they need to put in their lunch. At our house, we break it down into a main dish, fruit, vegetable, and snack type items.

- They can choose something from each category and stick each item in their lunch bag. Also, while making your grocery list each week, go over with your kid's lunch options in these categories what they'd like to "order" for that week.

- Small portions work great for school lunches. Kids will be more likely to eat apple slices than a whole apple placed in their lunch. Place apple slices in a bowl of half lemon juice and half water to soak a few minutes. This helps the apples not to brown.

- Make a list with your children on main course items they'd like. (That is what this cookbook is all about!) There are lots of great healthy lunch ideas to incorporate in your lunches beyond a sandwich.

- For snack items think nuts, cheese cubes, cheese sticks, yogurt, hard boiled eggs, jerky, soft pretzels, granola, trail mix and cereal mixes are all good choices.

- Plan ahead of time. You can freeze individual servings of dinner, hamburger rolls, soups, or other items your kids like that are precooked and they can take out the night before or morning. Muffins and quick breads are great for freezing too. You can bake a variety of flavors such as banana, zucchini, pumpkin, carrot, raisin, or apple. Store in individual servings in sandwich bags in the freezer.

- Buy small ice packs for placing into lunchboxes each morning. You can find these in decorative sizes and shapes now. Or freeze water bottles or juice boxes and add to school lunches. They will unthaw by lunch and keep things cool.

- Buy a child size thermos. You can send smoothies in them or soup. To warm a thermos, fill it with boiling water and seal the lid tight. Allow to sit 10 minutes. When ready to use pour out water and add the food. To cool the thermos, fill with ice cubes and seal tight. Let sit overnight. The next morning pour out water and fill. Close tightly. Make sure your child can open and close it!

- If you are using plastic containers for lunch items, make sure they will seal properly. Some of these containers if you shake upside down they will leak. Also make sure your child can open and close them properly so it won't leak after they eat.

- Give them a variety of things to choose from. Don't be afraid to give them something new sometimes. They might just be brave enough to try it when they are around their friends at school.

- The night before, after cleaning up from dinner, is the best time for packing school lunches. Put what items need to be chilled in the fridge and what items that don't, ready to go in the lunch box. Better yet, get your kids involved with making their lunches by having them do this step. This will save you some time in the morning.

- Finger foods are always a big hit with smaller kids and easy for them to eat than a large sandwich.

- If you want to avoid soggy bread in a sandwich, crackers make a good alternative. You can even separate crackers, cheese and meat into divided lunch containers. Much like the popular Lunchables you can buy in the grocery store. Homemade is always better.

Add some Vegetables to Lunch

Don't forget to provide vegetables in small containers to go in your kids lunch box. Talk with your kids and add what vegetables they would like to your "lunch list."

Some ideas could include:

- Mini green salads
- Carrots-cut in coins, sticks or diced
- Corn in a small container
- Green beans
- Steamed broccoli or raw
- Steamed cauliflower or raw
- Peas in a small container
- Bell pepper strips
- Cucumbers cut in coins or sticks

Make sure to include vegetables in their sandwiches or main dishes, as well as on the side in their lunch boxes. Get them involved in deciding which ones to include but try to get them to add at least one and work on adding more as they get use to it.

WRAPS AND ROLLS

Turkey Veggie Wrap

Roll up some of these crispy, flavor-loaded wraps for healthy school lunches, light supper or even sports meets.

Ingredients
4 whole wheat tortillas
2 cups grated carrot
8 fresh lettuce leaves, middle rib removed
1/2lb roasted deli turkey slices
1/3 cup mild salsa
2 tbsp. low-fat mayonnaise
1 red bell pepper, julienned
Ground pepper

Directions
Whisk together salsa and mayonnaise in small bowl.
Spread evenly 4 teaspoons of the mayonnaise mixture over the surface a tortilla.
Arrange two to three turkey slices over the tortilla and cover with two fresh leaves of lettuce.
Arrange grated carrots in a horizontal line on the lower third of the tortilla.
Place ¼ julienned red pepper on top of the grated carrots and season with ground pepper.
Starting from the bottom, roll up the tortilla, securing the filling to create a pleasing visual when cut.
Repeat the process with the remaining tortillas and other ingredients.

Spring Rolls
If desired add shredded chicken.
Ingredients:
round rice papers
snow pea sprouts, ends removed
Romaine lettuce, chopped
1 large carrot, cut into short thin strips
1 small red pepper, chopped into thin strips
1 cucumber, chopped into short thin strips
3 tbsp. fresh lime juice
1 1/2 tbsp. soy sauce
3 tbsp. Sweet Chilli Sauce
finely chopped unsalted roasted peanuts, optional

Directions

Prep the sauce by stirring together lime juice, soy sauce and chili sauce. Set aside.
Fill a large bowl halfway with warm water. Place one wrapper in the warm water until it's moistened about 15-20 seconds. Let drip water off and place on a cutting board or clean surface. Add diced ingredients to one end of the wrapper. Starting from the bottom, fold up the wrapper to enclose the filling tucking in the sides while you roll. When placing in your lunchbox, cover with a damp paper towel and place in a container or baggie. Add the sauce in a tightly covered container for dipping.

~You could replace the filling with any of these ideas:
shredded chicken, cooked
chopped pork, cooked
ground hamburger
chopped lettuce
shredded cabbage

finely chopped carrots
chopped cucumbers
bell peppers
mushrooms, chopped
cooked broccoli

Chicken Salad Rolls

We recommend you prepare this chicken salad the night before to allow the flavors to mesh.

Ingredients
1 cup chicken, shredded, cooked
2 whole-wheat hot dog buns or other bread of your choice
1/4 cup plain yogurt or mayonnaise
¼ small red onions, optional
1/3 cup anything chopped apples
spoonful of diced pickles, optional
Kosher salt
Freshly ground black pepper

Directions
Stir chicken mayonnaise, onions, apples and pickles together. Fill the buns evenly with the salad mix; wrap in parchment or waxed paper. Pack in lunch box. remember to include an ice pack.
If your kids don't like certain ingredients substitute what they do like such as; replace apples with celery or pickles with chopped cucumbers.

Taco Salad Wraps

Ingredients

1 can (15 1/2 ounces) can red kidney beans or black beans, washed and drained
6 (10-inch) flour tortillas
6 lettuce leaves, iceburg or Romaine, chopped
1 cup shredded cheddar cheese
3 tomatoes, seeded, cubed
2 tsp. olive oil
1/4 tsp. chili powder
1 tsp. ground cumin, or more to taste
1/2 tsp. salt
chopped olives

Directions

Mash together beans, cumin, olive oil, salt and chili powder until resembles refried beans.

Spread about 2 spoonfuls of refried beans onto each tortilla. Sprinkle top with shredded cheese, olives and diced tomato. Top with chopped lettuce and roll up tucking in edges as you roll.

Easy Peasy Lasagna Rolls

Ingredients
8 uncooked lasagna noodles
1 egg
12 oz container cottage cheese
1 Cup mozzarella cheese, shredded
1/4 Cup Parmesan cheese, grated
1/2 tsp dried basil
2 Cups of pasta sauce

Directions
Cook lasagna noodles in boiling water until tender. Allow to cool slightly until you can handle them.
In a small bowl, stir together cottage cheese, mozzarella, Parmesan and basil. Lay the lasagna noodles out flat. Spread sauce over the top of each noodle and top with cheese mixture. Roll up and place seam side down in a microwave safe dish. Microwave for 3-5 minutes until cheese is melted. Place in a lunch container and add a side of spaghetti sauce.
~ You can easily add chopped vegetables to the cheese mixture. Broccoli, cauliflower diced finely work great.

Scrambled Egg Burritos

Ingredients
2 large eggs
2 medium fat-free flour tortillas, heated
1 tbsp. low-fat milk
4 tbsp. shredded cheddar cheese (reduced-fat), divided
1/2 tsp. butter
Cooking spray
Black pepper, coarsely ground
1 tsp. chopped fresh cilantro
4 tbsp. tomato, chopped
1/8 tsp. kosher salt
2 tbsp. bottled chunky salsa, divided

Directions
In medium bowl, whisk eggs, milk, cilantro, salt and ground pepper.
Add butter to a skillet and melt butter. Pour in the egg mixture into the melted butter, and stir. Meanwhile, on each tortilla sprinkle with cheese and top with chopped tomatoes, and half of the scrambled eggs. Top with chunky salsa, if desired.
Starting from the bottom fold the tortilla up burrito style. Repeat the procedure with the remaining tortillas and ingredients. Wrap in parchment paper or wax paper and add to a lunchbox. These also freeze well.

Omelet Burrito

Ingredients

3 large eggs
1 tbsp. Butter
1/2 cup tomato salsa
1/2 cup grated Monterey Jack cheese
Salt
Ground black pepper
Avocado slices

Directions

Beat the eggs in a bowl and season with salt and ground pepper.
In a medium nonstick skillet, heat butter over medium. Pour the beaten eggs into the pan and cook like an omelet.
Top with cheese and spoon the salsa down the center of the cooked eggs.
Reduce the heat and let cheese melt completely.
Place the omelet on a sheet of waxed paper or parchment and roll up like a burrito and pack in the lunchbox with avocado slices.

Chicken Wraps

Ingredients
1 Cup sour cream
1 Cup mayonnaise
2 (1 oz.) envelopes of dry ranch dressing mix
4 Tablespoons vegetable oil
2 (16.2 oz.) cans refrigerated flaky biscuits
2 (6 oz.) pkg. cooked chicken strips
4 T of butter, melted

Directions
Blend together sour cream, mayonnaise and ranch dressing mix. Stir until well blended. On a cookie sheet spread a biscuit into an oval shape. Spread a spoonful of sour cream mixture over the biscuit. Add 2-3 chicken strips to the top and roll up tucking in edges. Brush each stuffed biscuit with melted butter and bake at 350 degrees for 20 minutes or until golden brown. Let cool and place in lunch containers or sandwich baggies.

Pizza Scrolls
Ingredients
salami, pepperoni or ham, finely chopped
1/2 finely chopped small red pepper
1/4 cup pizza sauce
1/2 cup grated mozzarella cheese
2 sheets readymade rolled puff pastry

Directions
Preheat the oven to 400 degrees F. In a bowl, stir together ham, chopped peppers and cheese. Spread each sheet of pastry with the pizza sauce, leaving a small border along one side. Sprinkle the ham mixture over the sauce. Starting from one side, firmly roll up the pastry to enclose the filling to form a log. Brush the edge lightly with a little water and press down firmly to seal the log. Using a serrated knife, cut each log into 1-inch circles and place each on a cookie sheet. Bake for about 15 to 20 minutes or until golden in color. Cool on a wire rack before packing in lunchboxes. These freeze well, so place extras in sandwich baggies for future lunches!
~Kids don't like red peppers? Replace with chopped carrots or chopped broccoli. I find the more you finely chop the vegetables, the kids don't mind as much.

Ham Salad Wrap

Ingredients

1-2 Tortillas per person
1 large slice of baked ham, diced small
2 tbsp sweet pickle relish or dill pickles, chopped finely
1/4-1/2 Cup mayonnaise or ranch salad dressing, depending on how creamy you like your ham salad

Directions

Blend together ham, relish and mayonnaise until well combined. Place on a tortilla circle and roll up. Wrap in plastic wrap or parchment paper. Place in lunchbox with a small ice pack.

Veggie Roll Me Ups

Ingredients
2 soft flour tortillas
2 Tablespoons cream cheese, softened
1 carrot, grated
1 sweet red pepper, chopped fine
handful cooked broccoli, chopped fine

Directions
Warm tortillas in the microwave by adding to a plate and warming for 10 seconds. Spread 1 tablespoon of cream cheese on both tortillas. Sprinkle top with carrot, pepper and broccoli. Roll tortilla around vegetables.

Try other vegetables your kids like or chopped lettuce or spinach leaves work well. You can also replace cream cheese with an herbed cream cheese for more flavor.

Ham and Apple Tortilla Wraps

Ingredients
2 apples, cored but not peeled
1 Cup water
2 Tablespoons lemon juice
3 Tablespoons mayonnaise style salad dressing
3 Tablespoons mustard
6 flour tortillas
12 slices deli style ham
12 slices American cheese
3 Cups chopped lettuce

Directions
Prepare a bowl of 1 Cup water and lemon juice. Slice apples into slices and add to lemon juice water. Lay a tortilla out flat and spread with mayonnaise and mustard. Layer ham, cheese and apple slices on top. Top with chopped lettuce. Roll tightly and wrap in plastic wrap.
Makes 6.

DIPS AND DIPPERS

Broccoli Dip

Ingredients

1 cup cottage cheese
1 14-ounce bag frozen broccoli, thawed
dash of salt
pita chips, vegetables cut into sticks, French bread slices, crackers, bagel slices or other dippers

Directions

In a food processor, blend broccoli, cheese and salt until smooth. Pack in a small sealable container with favorite "dippers".

White-Bean Dip
Ingredients
2 lb broccoli, cut into 1 1/2-inch-wide spears
2 1/2 tbsp. fresh lemon juice
3/4 cup silken tofu, gently rinsed and drained
1 (19-ounce) can white beans, rinsed and drained
1 garlic clove
1 tbsp. extra-virgin olive oil
1/4 tsp. ground cumin
Pinch of cayenne

Directions
Bring a pot of water to boil. Add a pinch of salt to the water. Blanch the broccoli spears by adding to the boiling water. Cook for 2 minutes. Drain and pour cold water over to stop the cooking process. Allow to dry several minutes.

Meanwhile prepare the dip, using a food processor blend garlic, lemon juice, tofu, white beans, olive oil cumin and cayenne pepper.

For school lunches, pack the dip in a sealable container with broccoli on the side for dipping.

Greek Yogurt Guacamole Dip

This healthy dip is easy to prepare and is a great snack for kids to carry to school. Pack with tortilla chips, pita chips or cut up veggies.

Ingredients:
2 ripe avocados, peeled, seeded
1/2 cup nonfat Greek yogurt
2 tbsp. fresh lime juice
3 tbsp. fresh cilantro, chopped
1/4 tsp. ground cumin
1 clove garlic, minced
Salt and ground black pepper, to taste
tortilla chips, pita chips, or cut up veggies, for serving

Directions:
In a food processor or blender, blend together all ingredients until smooth.
Pack in lunchboxes with tortilla chips, pita chips, or cut up veggies.
~If you like it spicy blend in 1 tbsp. jalapeño pepper, seeded, finely chopped

Skillet Nacho Dip
Ingredients
1 lb. lean ground beef
1 small onion, chopped or grated
1 (19 oz.) can tomato soup
1 (15 oz.) can chili beans, do not drain
1 (4.5 oz.) can green chilies, chopped, optional
1 Cup frozen whole kernel corn
1 (4 oz.) bag Cheddar cheese, shredded

Directions
Cook ground beef and chopped onions until no longer pink. Drain. Stir in tomato soup, chili beans with their juice, green chilies and cor. Stir well. Bring to a boil and cook about 10 minutes until thickens. Add to lunch containers or thermos and serve with a side of cheese and tortilla or corn chips if desired.
~You can also add toppings such as sour cream or diced olives depending on your children tastes.

Baked Onion Dip

Ingredients
1 cup mayonnaise
1 cup grated Swiss cheese
1 tbsp. grated Parmesan cheese
1 cup sweet onions, grated or finely chopped
1/4 tsp. garlic powder
1/4 tsp. garlic salt

Directions
In a 1-quart baking dish combine all the ingredients and bake at 325°F for about 40 minutes, uncovered. Pack in lunchboxes with crackers, chips or bread.

Chicken Fingers with Honey-Mustard Sauce

Ingredients
Chicken
1/4 cup breadcrumbs, seasoned
16-20 chicken breast tenders
1 tbsp. minced onion
1/2 cup cornflakes, coarsely crushed
1/2 cup of buttermilk
1 tbsp. vegetable oil
1/4 tsp. black pepper
1/4 tsp. dried thyme
1 tsp. paprika

Directions
Preheat your oven to 400 degrees F.
Place chicken in a bowl and pour buttermilk over the top. Let sit 10-15 minutes.
In a gallon size plastic bag, combine cornflakes, onion, breadcrumbs, paprika, thyme, and pepper; add four chicken pieces at a time. Seal the bag and shake to coat the chicken with cornflake mixture. Place on a large cookie sheet. Repeat the process with the remaining chicken pieces. Bake 15-20 minutes until golden brown and no longer pink. Meanwhile, prepare sauce by combining 1/4 cup spicy brown mustard and 1/4 cup honey. Blend together and place in small plastic containers. Once chicken is cooked allow to cool and pack in lunch boxes with the sauce.
~For an easy school morning, make these the night before and freeze extras for another day.

Edamame Hummus
Ingredients
1 1/2 cup edamame, shelled, cooked and chilled
1 tsp. soy sauce
1/4 Cup tahini paste
2 – 3 tbsp. olive oil
2 tbsp. sesame or sesame oil
1 clove garlic
Juice of 1 lemon
pinch of salt to taste

Directions
In a food processor, blend cooked edamame, soy sauce, lemon juice, garlic, salt, sesame oil, and water until well blended. Then add in olive oil and continue pulsing the processor until the dip's consistency is soft. If too thick, blend in 1-2 Tablespoons of water. Pack in small containers and serve with crackers, pita chips or vegetable slices.

Veggies and Pizza Dip
Ingredients
2 (10.5 oz) cans prepared pizza sauce
2 Tablespoons cornstarch
1/4 lb. pepperoni, chopped fine
1 tsp. oregano
16 oz. processed cheese spread, cubed, such as Velvetta
1 Tablespoon dried parsley
1 tsp. minced onion
1/2 tsp. hot pepper sauce, if desired
dippers: carrot sticks, fresh mushrooms, cherry tomatoes, bell pepper strips, and/or celery sticks, French bread slices

Directions
In a microwave safe bowl, add cornstarch and pizza sauce. Blend together and cook 2 minutes. Take out of microwave and add cheese cubes. Continue to cook in the microwave for 1-minute intervals stirring each time until cheese is melted. Stir in meat and oregano. Add parsley and hot pepper sauce. Place dip in small containers and serve as a dip with the vegetables.
~If kids like Italian sausage replace the pepperoni with it.

Salsa Bean Dip

Ingredients
1/4 cup refried beans
1 1/2 tsp. chopped fresh cilantro, optional
1 tbsp. salsa
1-ounce tortilla chips, (about 10)
other additions could be chopped onions, chopped olives, whatever your kids like

Directions
In a bowl, combine the refried beans, cilantro, salsa, and any other additions. Pack dip in small container with tortilla chips on the side.

Black Bean & Tomato Salsa

Adding the canned beans to a spicy salsa is one of the best ways of boosting fiber as well as improving nutritional value of your kids' meals. Prepare this healthy salsa and pack with scrambled egg burritos or mini hamburgers.

Ingredients
1 cup canned black beans, rinsed
1 cup plum tomatoes (3 medium tomatoes), seeded and diced
2 -3 tbsp. taco seasoning, based on your preference for heat
1/2 cup fresh parsley or cilantro, chopped
1 green pepper, chopped
1 (4 ounce) can green chilies, drained
1/8 tsp. salt
1/21 yellow onion, chopped

Directions
In a medium bowl, combine all the ingredients and stir to blend well.
 Chill before packing in lunchboxes with burgers or scrambled egg burritos.

Feta & Herb Dip

Lots of freshly chopped herbs add zing to this delicious bean dip. The dip is great when packed with assorted veggies such as snow peas, radishes, bell pepper strips, baby carrots, cauliflower florets and broccoli.

Ingredients
1 15-ounce can white beans, rinsed
1 tbsp. lemon juice
1/2 cup crumbled feta cheese
3/4 cup nonfat plain yogurt
1/4 cup fresh dill, chopped
1/4 cup chopped fresh parsley
dash of salt and pepper
1/4 cup fresh chives, chopped or 1 tsp dried chives

Directions
Add beans, lemon juice, feta, yogurt, garlic salt and pepper in a food processor or blender and blend until smooth. Add fresh dill, chives, and parsley, and continue pureeing until all blended together. Place in small container and serve with vegetables in lunchboxes.

Spinach Veggie Dip

Ingredients

10 oz chopped spinach, frozen
2 Cups mayonnaise
1/2 Cup fresh parsley, chopped
1/2 Cup green onion, chopped
dash of salt and pepper
Assorted vegetables cut up; carrot or celery sticks, broccoli, cauliflower or even cherry tomatoes.

Directions

Cook spinach according to package directions. Drain and place on paper towel. Squeeze water out of spinach as much as possible. Add to bowl and blend in mayonnaise, chopped parsley and chopped onions. Season with salt and pepper. Blend until all ingredients are well combined. Place the dip into a prepared cooled thermos or lunch container. Add cut vegetables in a separate container.

Easy Lunchbox Apples

Ingredients
1 apple
1-2 Tablespoons lemon juice
1-2 Cups water

Directions
Mix together lemon juice and water. Cut apple in slices and let soak in lemon water several minutes. Place in container or baggie and serve with dip or yogurt of choice. (The next page has a good fruit dip)

~Don't like the taste of the apples in lemon water. Add 1/2 teaspoon salt to 4 Cups of water and soak your apples in salty water instead.

~Or soak in pineapple juice

Creamy Fruit Dip
Ingredients
8 oz. cream cheese, softened
3 Tablespoons sugar
1 Cup sour cream
1 tsp vanilla
fruit slices, apples, strawberries, kiwi

Directions
Blend together soft cream cheese, sugar, sour cream and vanilla until well combined. Place in small lunch containers and place in lunches with a sliced fruit assortment or fruit salad.

Cinnamon Yogurt Snack Dip

Ingredients
3 Tablespoons vanilla yogurt
2 tsp honey
dash of cinnamon

Directions
Stir in honey and cinnamon into vanilla. Store in a thermos or lunch container.
Chill overnight. Serve with graham crackers or apple slices.

Main Dishes with Veggies

Lunchtime Sloppy Joe

Ingredients
1 lb ground beef
1 small onion, chopped
1 small green pepper, chopped
3/4 C ketchup
1 tsp yellow mustard
3 tsp brown sugar
1/2 tsp garlic powder
1/2 tsp salt
1/4 tsp pepper

Directions
Brown the ground beef and in a skillet with the chopped onions and green peppers. Drain off fat and place back into skillet. Add ketchup, mustard, and brown sugar. Season with garlic powder, salt and pepper. Turn to low heat and cook about 15-20 minutes until cooked through. Add to lunch containers or thermos. Place a hamburger bun in a baggie or crackers for dipping. This recipe freezes well for future lunches.
~If your kids don't like green peppers try red or yellow and finely dice. Once cooked in the sauce it is hard to see. Chopped carrots also work well.

Stir Fry Thermos Lunch
Ingredients
1 tbsp olive oil + extra if needed
1 small zucchini, sliced in rounds
1 small onion, wedged
small can sliced mushrooms, drained
1 small red sweet pepper, cut into strips
2 Cup fresh bean sprouts
1 Tablespoon soy sauce
dash pepper

Directions
Place the olive oil into a wok and heat several minutes. Add chopped zucchini and onion and cook until tender about 3-5 minutes. Set aside in bowl. Sauté mushrooms and red pepper strips about 2 minutes. Blend in the onion mixture. Add bean sprouts to the wok. If pan is too dry, add 1 Tablespoon more oil.
Blend in the soy sauce and a dash of pepper. Cook about 5 minutes until stirring occasionally, or until completely heated through. Place immediately into a warm prepared thermos.

Easy Spaghetti with Sauce
Ingredients
1-pound spaghetti
pinch of sugar, if desired
28 oz. can whole tomatoes, puree in blender if your kids don't like the tomato chunks
2 cloves garlic, finely minced
2 tbsp. olive oil and extra for drizzling
Parmesan cheese
1/2 tsp. salt
dash pepper

Directions
In a large pot, boil water for spaghetti and cook spaghetti until el dente.
In a skillet, sauté garlic in olive oil. Add in sugar, tomatoes and, salt and black pepper.
Bring to a boil and reduce heat. Simmer for 15-20 minutes.
Stir spaghetti and sauce together. Add to thermos or food containers and drizzle with olive oil, if desired.
Top with parmesan cheese or mozzarella cheese.

Layered Eggplant Lunch

Ingredients
3 tbsp oil
1 small eggplant, sliced
2 potatoes, skin left on and sliced
1 onion, sliced
1 green bell pepper, cut into strips
1 large tomato, sliced
1 garlic clove, minced
1/2 tsp each parsley and basil

Directions
Warm oil in a skillet and add eggplant and potatoes layered on the bottom of the skillet. Add onion to the top, then peppers and tomatoes. Sprinkle w with garlic, parsley and basil. Allow the layers to simmer in the hot oil for 20 minutes.
Do not add any water, lower heat if cooking too quickly. Cook with lid on15 minutes. Spoon out layers of vegetables and add to a thermos.
~If your kids like, sprinkle a little parmesan cheese over the top before eating.

Chili Mac Supper

Ingredients

1 Cup uncooked macaroni
1 lb. lean ground beef
1/2 tsp chili powder
1 (11.25 oz.) can chili beef soup
1 (14.5 oz.) can diced tomatoes
1/2 C of cheddar cheese, shredded

Directions

Cook pasta until al dente. Drain and set aside. Meanwhile, crumble ground beef in a skillet and brown until no longer pink. Drain and add meat back to skillet. Stir in chili powder, soup and tomatoes with their juice. Stir in the cooked pasta. Cook the mixture about 10 minutes or until heated through, stirring often. Place in lunch containers or thermos. Pack a side of cheese for the topping.

~You can pack a little container of sour cream and a sprinkle of green onions, if desired.

Sesame Noodles
Ingredients
1-pound thin spaghetti or angel hair pasta
1 zucchini, peeled and diced
2 tbsp. toasted sesame oil
1/3 cup rice vinegar
1/3 cup soy sauce
1/2 tsp. red-pepper flakes
1 to 2 garlic cloves
2 medium carrots, peeled and shredded or diced small
1 Tablespoon sesame seeds, add more if you'd like

Directions
Follow the package instructions to cook pasta in large pot of boiling salted water.
Drain and transfer to large bowl.
In the meantime, prepare sauce by blending sesame oil, vinegar, soy sauce, pepper flakes, and garlic until smooth.
Place the cooked pasta into large bowl and toss with the diced zucchini, carrots and sauce.

Peanut Sauce Spaghetti
Ingredients
8 ounces whole-wheat spaghetti
2 tbsp. brown sugar
3 tbsp. peanut butter
1 container (14 ounces) firm tofu, drained and cut into 1-inch cubes
3 medium carrots, halved, and cut into thin strips or diced finely
4 ounces snow peas, cut ends off
2 tbsp. rice vinegar
2 tbsp. soy sauce

Directions
Follow the package instructions to cook pasta in a pot of boiling salted water until al dente. Reserve half cup of water.
Before draining, add tofu, snow peas and carrots to the pot. Let cook another 2-3 minutes. Drain the pasta mixture immediately; set aside.
In small jar or quart measuring cup, blend the sauce ingredients together including vinegar, soy sauce, peanut butter and sugar.
Add the sauce to the pasta mixture and stir until sauce covers the noodles.
Add the reserved pasta water in small amounts at a time to make a thin sauce to coat the spaghetti. Add to lunch containers or thermos.

Gnocchi with Marinara

Ingredients

3-4 Cups homemade or store bough potato gnocchi, cooked
3/4 cup ricotta cheese
1/2 cup spaghetti sauce
dash salt and pepper to taste
1/4 cup grated Parmesan, topping or mozzarella balls

Directions

Boil gnocchi according to package directions. Preheat oven to 400 degrees F. Add all ingredients except parmesan to a shallow casserole dish. Cook on high heat until gnocchi start to brown. Before serving add either mozzarella balls or Parmesan cheese. Place in a thermos or lunch container.

Veggie Burgers

Ingredients

1 (15.5-ounce) can pinto beans, washed and drained
1/2 cup bulgur
1 large egg, lightly beaten
1/2 cup Swiss cheese, grated
1 scallion, thinly sliced
1/2 cup carrots, finely grated
1 tbsp. olive oil
salt and ground pepper to taste
chopped lettuce
4 buns

Directions

In large bowl, combine one cup of boiling water and bulgur.
Cover the bowl and let sit for 30 minutes or until bulgur is tender.
Strain any remaining water off bulgur and place in a bowl.
In a blender or food processor, puree the pinto beans. Add the beans to bulgur as well as the egg, scallion, carrots, and Swiss cheese. Season with salt and ground pepper and mix to combine well.
In large nonstick skillet, heat oil over medium heat. Add half cup of the bean mixture and flatten with the back of the spatula.
Makes about 4 patties. Pack the burgers in a lunch container with buns and lettuce.

Easy Taco Pie

I don't usually use Bisquick mix but this recipe works well. If you'd like you can leave Bisquick off or replace with a pie crust on the top and/or bottom. *

Ingredients
1 lb lean ground beef
3/4 cup tomato, chopped
3/4 cup Cheddar cheese or Monterey Jack
1/2 cup Bisquick® mix
1 cup milk
2 eggs
1 (4.5-oz) can chopped and drained green chilies, optional
1 (1-oz) package taco seasoning mix
1 medium onion, chopped
Sour cream, if desired
Salsa, if desired
1 1/2 cups lettuce, shredded, if desired

Directions
Preheat oven to 400 degrees F. Spray a pie plate and set aside.
Cook ground beef and onions in skillet until no longer pink. Drain. Stir in seasoning mix.
Add beef into bottom of pie plate. Top with chilies.
*Stir milk, eggs and Bisquick mix in a small bowl to mix well. Pour the mixture into the pie plate. Bake in oven for about 20-25 minutes. Top the pie with tomato and cheese and place in the oven just until cheese melts. Let cool before adding to lunch containers.
Pack in lunch boxes with any toppings they like. Try other toppings such as guacamole, chopped black olives, sliced green onions, shredded lettuce, or crushed corn chips, whatever your kids love most!

Tortellini with Peas

Ingredients

1 (9 oz.) pkg. cheese ravioli or Tortellini
1 Cup frozen peas
2 Tablespoons flour
1/8 teaspoon pepper
1 Cup half and half
1 can diced tomatoes, pureed if your kids don't like the chunks
dash salt and pepper
2 Tablespoons Parmesan cheese, grated

Directions

Cook tortellini or ravioli in boiling water until tender. During the last few minutes, add frozen peas and drain.
Meanwhile, blend half and half, pureed tomatoes, flour, salt and pepper together in a saucepan. Cook and stir several minutes until thickens. Toss sauce with ravioli and peas. Sprinkle with Parmesan cheese and serve.

Corn and Beef Hash

Ingredients
1 tbsp canola oil
1 lb ground beef
2 C frozen corn, thawed
2 Cups canned beans, whichever type your kids like, pinto, white, black, etc.

Directions
Cook ground beef in skillet until no longer pink and drain. Add back to skillet and stir in corn and beans. Bring mixture to low and cook about 10-15 minutes. Place in warm thermos or food container. Serve with corn chips, tortilla or pita chips.

Tuna Vegetable Alfredo
Ingredients
3 Cups pasta noodles
2 Cups broccoli florets
1 red sweet pepper, cut into strips, optional
1 (10 oz.) container of Alfredo sauce
1 (9.5) oz. can of tuna, drained

Directions
Cook pasta according to the package directions. Add broccoli and sweet peppers the last 5 minutes of the cooking time. Drain well and return to the pan. Pour the Alfredo sauce into the pan and stir to combine. Fold in the tuna. Cook the mixture for 5 minutes or until heated through.
Add to lunch containers or thermos

Beans and Rice Thermos Meal
Ingredients
1/2 Cup canned black beans
1/2 Cup canned corn, drained
1/2 Cup brown rice, cooked
1/4 Cup salsa

Directions
Warm beans and corn in a microwave safe bowl. Add in cooked rice and stir in salsa. Stir until well combined. Cook in microwave bowl for about 5 minutes until heated through.
Place in a prepared warm thermos.

Easiest Mac and Cheese

This recipe is great for cooking the night before and bringing leftovers to school the next day.

Ingredients

8 oz. Macaroni elbows

8 oz. Colby or cheddar cheese cubed, or combination of cheeses

24 oz. can 100% Tomato juice with no sugar or V8 Juice

Directions

Add macaroni, cheese, and tomato juice in a casserole dish. Bake in a 350 F oven for 30-45 minutes. Stir well and that is all there is to it!

SOUPS

Chicken Noodle Soup with Spinach

Kids love chicken and pasta, and sneaking in a little antioxidant-dense spinach will make this meal very nutritious.

Ingredients
1 (5-ounce) package baby spinach
1/2 cup small shape pasta, uncooked
1/4 tsp. grated whole nutmeg
2 tsp. olive oil
1/4 tsp. ground black pepper
1/4 tsp. salt
2 chicken-breast, skinless, boneless
6 Cups chicken broth
1 garlic clove, minced
1/4 cup Parmesan cheese

Directions
Sauté garlic in large pot. Add in whole chicken breasts, nutmeg, and broth. Add a dash of salt and pepper. Bring the mixture to boil and reduce heat to medium. Simmer for 10-15 minutes.
 Remove chicken from the soup and set aside to cool. Increase heat to soup and bring to a boil. Add in pasta and simmer 5-8 minutes until pasta is tender.
Shred or slice the chicken breasts and return to the soup. Stir in spinach leaves and simmer until wilted about 1 minute.
Add to plastic containers or thermos and sprinkle the top with Parmesan cheese.

Quick Microwave Tomato Soup

Ingredients
1/4 to 1/3 cup cream
1 to 2 tsp. fresh lemon juice
1 Tbsp. brown sugar
1 cup chicken broth
1 rib celery, roughly chopped
1 (28-ounce) can whole tomatoes, in juice
Kosher salt
Freshly ground black pepper

Directions
Blend the broth, celery and tomatoes in a blender until smooth.
Season the mixture with salt and ground pepper to taste. Stir in the cream.
Add tomato mixture into a microwave-safe bowl and microwave on high for about 4 minutes or until heated through. Pour soup into an air-tight thermos while it is hot and it will stay warm by the kids lunchtime.

Italian Pasta Soup

Ingredients:
1 lb. ground beef
2 (14 oz.) cans of beef broth
1 (16 oz.) pkg. frozen broccoli and cauliflower or variety of vegetables
1 (14.5 oz.) can diced tomatoes
1/2 Cup tomato juice
1 Cup pasta, uncooked, any shape
1/2 Cup basil pesto

Directions:
In a soup pot, brown ground beef until no longer pink. Drain and place back in soup pot
Add in broth, vegetables, tomatoes with their juice and tomato juice. Bring to a boil and add in pasta. Cover with a lid and reduce heat. Simmer about 10 minutes until vegetables are tender and pasta is cooked. Take off stove and stir in pesto. Pack into lunch containers or thermos. Add a slice of bread or crackers for the kids lunch to go with the soup.
~If you don't have basil pesto on hand that's okay. Just add a pinch of dried basil to the soup before bringing it to a boil.

Ham Pea Soup That Kids actually like!

Ingredients
3 tbsp canola oil
2 garlic cloves, minced
1 onion, chopped
1 stalk celery, chopped
1 (15 oz) can peas
6 Cups chicken broth
1 bay leaf
2 oz ham, diced
3 potatoes, peeled and cubed
3 carrots, chopped
dash of pepper and salt, if needed

Directions
Using a soup pan, sauté garlic, onion and chopped celery in oil, several minutes until softened. Pour in chicken broth, peas, and bay leaf. Add in diced ham. Cover and cook over medium heat about 1 hour or until the peas are soft.
Add the potatoes and carrots. Cover with a lid and simmer 20 minutes.
If the soup too thick, stir in 1/4 Cup water or broth at a time until desired consistency.
Pour into a warm thermos or lunch container.
~Freezes well, too!

Steak and Onion Soup

Ingredients
1 tbsp canola oil
1 lb round steak, cut into 1-inch cubes
1 tbsp butter
3 medium onions, sliced into rings
6 Cups beef broth
1 tbsp Dijon style mustard
1 tsp. salt
1/2 tsp pepper
1 (6 oz) can sliced mushrooms, drained
1 Tablespoon dried parsley
1 Cup Swiss cheese, shredded

Directions
In a large soup pot, heat oil. Add steak cut into cubes and sauté until browned on all sides. Set aside. Add butter to pot and melt. Add chopped onions and mushrooms. Cook until onions are translucent. Pour in the beef broth.
Blend mustard into broth. Sprinkle in the parsley, salt and pepper. Add steak cubes back into the pot.
Bring soup to a boil and turn to low and cover with a lid. Let simmer 40 minutes.
Place the heat on medium high and bring the mixture to a quick boil.
Place the heat back on low and cover the kettle. Cook the soup 45 minutes. Just before serving add shredded Swiss cheese or other cheese your kids like.
For packed lunches pour hot soup into a thermos or allow to cool slightly before pouring into lunch containers.
~Another soup that freezes well.

Corn, Sausage and Potato Soup
Ingredients

1 lb breakfast sausage links, cut into bite size pieces, optional

3 cups frozen hash brown potatoes or use 3 potatoes peeled and cubed

1 can (15 oz) creamed corn, undrained

1 can (10 oz) cream celery soup

1 can whole corn undrained

4 cups water

pinch of salt and pepper

Directions

In a soup pan, add potatoes, corn and canned soup. Add in water and sausage cut into bite size pieces. Stir to combine. Season with salt and pepper. Pack in lunch containers or thermos.

Chicken Chowder

Ingredients
1 tbsp canola oil
1 onion, chopped fine
2 tbsp flour
1 1/2 Cup milk
1 Cup frozen hash browns
1 Cup corn, frozen
3/4 Cup chicken breast, cooked and cubed
dash of salt and pepper

Directions
Heat oil and sauté onion until translucent. Stir in flour. Add milk and bring to a boil, stirring constantly. Whisk together for 1-2 minutes until mixture starts to thicken. Add potatoes and corn. Bring t o a boil. Then reduce heat to low. Cover and cook about 10-12 minutes until potatoes are tender. Add in cooked cubed or shredded chicken. Heat an additional 10 minutes. Add to a thermos or food container.

Ham Macaroni and Cheese Chowder

Ingredients

1 (14 oz.) can of chicken broth
1 Cup of water
1 Cup of pasta
1 Cup frozen corn
1 Cup cooked ham, diced
6 oz. of American cheese, cubed
1 Cup milk

Directions

In a soup pan, add chicken broth and water. Bring to a boil and in pasta. Simmer about 10 minutes until pasta is tender. Do not drain. Stir in corn, cheese cubes and ham. Then add in milk. Stir until well blended and cook until cheese is melted.
Add to lunch containers or thermos.

Pepperoni Pizza Soup

Ingredients

2 tsp canola oil
1 small onion, chopped fine
1 clove of garlic, crushed
1 (6 oz) can sliced mushrooms, drained
1 small green pepper, chopped fine
1 (15 oz) pkg. pepperoni slices, diced
1 Cup beef broth
2 (14 oz) cans diced tomatoes
1 tsp basil
1 tsp oregano

Directions

In a soup pot, heat oil. Add onions and garlic and sauté about 3-5 minutes. Add in beef broth, mushrooms, green peppers and pepperoni. Add the diced tomatoes, basil and oregano. Cover and cook the soup on medium for about 15- 20 minutes.

For your kids lunchbox, add a small container on the side with shredded mozzarella or Parmesan cheese.

Chicken Taco Soup

Ingredients

2 slices of bacon
1 (6 oz) can sliced mushrooms, drained
1 small onion, chopped
1 small red pepper, chopped
4 C chicken broth
2 C chicken breast, cooked and chopped
2 C taco salsa
1 tbsp taco seasoning

Directions

Cook bacon until crisp. Allow to cool and crumble. In a soup pot, sauté mushrooms, onion and red pepper in with the crumbled bacon. Add chicken broth to vegetables. Add the chopped chicken to the broth. Stir in salsa and taco seasoning. Bring to a boil. Then turn heat to low and simmer 15 minutes. Pour into a prepared thermos.

Add a small container with cheese and/or sour cream to eat with their lunch.

SALADS

Mediterranean Tuna Salad

You may want to skip the mayo and instead dress with olive oil.

Ingredients

1 head shredded romaine lettuce
1 bunch sliced green onions, if desired
2 pieces naan or pita bread
1 cucumber, diced
1 14-ounce can chickpeas, rinsed and drained
1 12-ounce can solid tuna in water, drained, flaked
1/4 cup fresh dill, chopped or 1 Tablespoon dried dill
1/3 cup olive oil, and extra for brushing
Grated zest and juice of 1 lemon
2 tsp. Dijon mustard
1-pint grape or cherry tomatoes, halved
dash salt and ground pepper

Directions

In small bowl, blend together lemon juice, lemon zest and mustard.
Gently whisk in olive oil to blend well. Stir in the dill, salt and ground pepper to taste. Set aside.
In medium bowl, toss scallions, cucumber, chickpeas, tuna and tomatoes with quarter cup of the dressing. Season with some salt and ground pepper.
Toss the romaine with the remaining half of the dressing.
Top with the tuna salad and pack in lunch boxes with the pita or naan bread.

Tuna Pasta Salad

Ingredients

1 (8 oz) box large spiral pasta
1 (15 oz) can four bean mix, drained
6 cherry tomatoes, quartered
1/4 Cup sweet pickles, chopped
1 (7.5 oz) can tuna in water, drained and flaked
1/4 Cup mayonnaise
2 tsp white vinegar
1 tsp parsley, chopped fine

Directions

Cook the pasta as directed on the package. Rinse under cold water and drain well.

Place the pasta in a large bowl and add the four-bean mix, quartered tomatoes and pickles. Add in the tuna. In a separate bowl, mix together the mayonnaise, vinegar and parsley until smooth.

Pour over the top of the pasta mixture. Stir together until well coated. Place in a pre-chilled thermos and include an ice pack in the lunchbox.

Pepper Bow Tie Pasta

Ingredients
8 oz. of uncooked bow tie pasta
12 oz. Italian sausage links, cut into 1 in pieces
2 red sweet peppers, diced
1/2 Cup beef broth
1/4 tsp pepper

Directions
Cook pasta until al dente. In a skillet, add sausage and peppers. Sauté about 5 minutes until peppers are tender. Drain off or carefully wipe with a paper towel fat from skillet. Pour beef broth into skillet and allow to cook 5 minutes. In a bowl, mix together pasta, peppers, sausage and broth. Stir to combine. Place in lunch containers or thermos.

Makes 4 servings

Colorful Fruit Salad

Ingredients
1 Cup fruit cocktail, drained
1 Cup chunked pineapple, drained
1 Cup mandarin oranges, drained
1 Cup sour cream
1 Cup rainbow miniature marshmallows

Directions
Mix together all ingredients together in a large mixing bowl. Gently stir the sour cream to coat the fruit.
Place in a pre-chilled thermos or in a lunch container and let sit in the fridge overnight. Include an ice pack in the lunchbox, also.

Easy Chef's Salad

Ingredients
1 head of lettuce, shredded
2 tomatoes, chopped
1 cucumber, sliced thin
4 hard boiled eggs, chopped
4 slices of deli chicken cut into thin strips
4 slices of deli turkey cut into thin strips
1 (8 oz.) pkg. mild cheddar cheese, shredded

Directions
Place the lettuce into a large salad bowl.
Add the tomatoes and cucumbers and toss to combine.
Spread the chopped egg over the top.
Add the chicken and turkey slices and top with the shredded cheese.
~Let kids add any of their favorites including leftover fresh veggies, diced ham or diced steak and don't forget the dressings in a small container.

No Cabbage Cole Slaw

Ingredients

1 (8 oz) pkg. broccoli coleslaw mix
1 (4 oz) bottle of coleslaw dressing or other dressing of your choice
1 (4 oz) pkg. dried cranberries or raisins
1/2 Cup almonds or pistachio nuts
dash of salt and pepper

Directions

In a large bowl, add broccoli coleslaw mix and add dressing. Stir to coat. Add in the cranberries and nuts. Season with salt and pepper. Cover and refrigerate until ready to place into your pre-chilled thermos.

Salad Shaker
Ingredients
1 Cup of torn salad greens
2 Tablespoons carrot, grated
1/4 Cup of cooked chicken, cubed
broccoli or other vegetables you like chopped finely
2 tbsp cheddar cheese, shredded
sprinkle of sunflower seeds or chopped almonds, optional

Directions
Place the salad greens into a bowl with a tight-fitting lid.
Spread the carrot over the top of the greens.
Add the chicken and sprinkle with the cheddar cheese.
Cover the bowl and shake until all the ingredients are mixed together well.
Top with your favorite dressing before eating.
~Kids can add any of their favorite salad ingredients like tomatoes or chopped hardboiled egg.
Makes 1 salad

Fruity Rice Salad

Ingredients

1 Cup microwave basmati rice, cooked and cooled
small drizzle honey about 1/2 teaspoon
1/4 Cup raisins
1 tbsp. olive oil
1 lemon, zest and a spoonful of juice
1/4 Cup low-fat cheese, cubed
1/4 Cup chopped sliced ham
1/4 Cup frozen peas
1 apple cored and cubed
1/2 tsp Dijon mustard

Directions

In a bowl, combine sliced ham, apple, cheese cubes, raisins, and cooked rice. Whisk together honey, Dijon mustard, olive oil, and a spoonful of lemon juice in a small bowl. Pour this mixture over the rice salad, stir to combine well and chill before packing.

Ramen Turkey Slaw

Ingredients

1 (16 oz.) pkg. shredded coleslaw mix
6 oz. cooled turkey breast, cubed
1 (3 oz.) pkg. ramen noodles
1/2 Cup vinaigrette salad dressing
1 (11 oz.) can mandarin oranges, drained well

Directions

In a large bowl, add coleslaw mix and add turkey. Crumble the ramen noodles into the slaw and reserve the seasoning packet for another use. Pour the dressing over the salad and toss to coat the slaw well. Fold in the oranges.

Makes 4 servings

Smoked Salmon and Pasta in Lemon Cream Sauce

Many kids hate seafood, so try slipping some salmon into this hearty and creamy pasta. Since the salmon you'll use in this recipe is smoked, it doesn't have more of a "fishy" taste and will blend perfect with the sour cream-based sauce.

Ingredients

12 ounces pasta, any shape
4 ounces smoked salmon, thinly sliced
1 (10-ounce) bag frozen peas
1/2 Cup sour cream
1 Cup vegetable broth
2 large green onions, finely chopped
2 tbsp. fresh lemon juice
1 tbsp. olive oil
dash of salt and pepper

Directions

Follow the package instructions to cook the pasta. Drain and reserve 1/4 cup cooking water in a bowl. In same pan heat oil and sauté green onions. Add broth and let cook on medium about 10 minutes. Take off heat and blend in sour cream, pasta, and 1/4 reserved cooking water. Add lemon juice and let sit about 5 minutes to cool slightly. Season with salt and pepper. For lunchboxes, place in containers or a thermos.

Crunchy Romaine Berry Salad
Ingredients
1 package ramen noodles, save seasoning packet for another use
2 cups fresh strawberries, sliced or raspberries
1 cup almonds, chopped
8 cups romaine lettuce, chopped
1/4 cup butter

Dressing:
1/2 tsp. soy sauce
1/4 cup sugar
2 tbsp. white wine vinegar
1/4 cup canola oil

Directions
Crumble noodles into small pieces. In large skillet, melt butter. Cook almonds and Ramen noodles about 10 minutes or until golden. Set aside.
Mix together the dressing ingredients
For packed lunches mix together in lunch containers lettuce and strawberries. Add a small side container with noodles and nut mixture and another with dressing. Packing separately will help the noodles stay crunchy.

Greek Salad

Ingredients

2 cups romaine lettuce, chopped
1 medium tomato, diced
1/2 cup cucumber, peeled and diced
1 tsp. dried oregano
2 tbsp. fat-free vinaigrette dressing or other oil/vinegar dressing of choice
1/2 cup croutons
1 tbsp. crumbled feta cheese
3 pitted Kalamata olives, chopped

Directions

In a lunch container add lettuce, tomato, cucumber, oregano, feta cheese and olives. Add dressing in a small container and croutons in a separate sandwich baggie or container.

Ham and Cheese Tortellini Salad
Ingredients:
2 Cup frozen cheese filled tortellini
1 1/2 Cup cooked ham, cut into strips
1 Cup of cheddar cheese cubes
1/2 bell pepper, diced
1 Cup broccoli florets
1/2 Cup Italian salad dressing
1 tbsp Parmesan cheese, grated
Lettuce, chopped
4 tomatoes cut in quarters

Directions
Cook the tortellini per directions on the package. When done drain and rinse with cold water. Add to bowl. Stir in ham, cheese cubes, broccoli and peppers with the tortellini.
Pour dressing over the salad and stir to combine. Sprinkle with Parmesan cheese and let chill overnight. Before packing add chopped lettuce to bottom of lunch container. Add chilled salad to the top of the lettuce.
~Use whichever vegetables your kids like; cauliflower, cooked squash cubes, olives, etc.

Middle Eastern Salad

Ingredients
2 pita bread
small container of grape tomatoes
2 Lebanese cucumbers, diced
2 radishes, thinly sliced
2 tsp. sesame seeds
1 tbsp. lemon juice
1/4 Cup olive oil
1 Tablespoons parsley
salt and pepper to taste

Directions
Preheat oven to 400-degree F. Place pita bread on cookie sheet, brush with oil and sprinkle with salt and sesame seeds. Place in warmed oven for about 7-10 minutes or until crispy. Remove and set aside.
With a vegetable peeler cut cucumber in ribbons. In lunch container, add cucumber ribbons, tomatoes and radishes.
Mix together oil, parsley and lemon juice. Season with salt and pepper. Pack in small containers.
Break pita bread into bite size pieces and place in a side container or sandwich baggie.

Sweet Lunchbox Noodles

This recipe provides the perfect way to utilize some leftovers. It's an ideal lunchbox recipe for your kids.

Ingredients

3/4 cup small pasta, cooked
3 tsp. cheese, shredded
1/4 cup crushed pineapple, not drained

Directions

In a lunch container or small thermos, add cooked pasta, cheese and pineapple. Blend together until well combined.

Pasta and Broccoli Salad

Ingredients

2 cups broccoli florets
1 cup pasta, whichever shape you have on hand
2 tbsp. olive oil
1/4 cup grated Parmesan
Salt and pepper
Lemon wedge, (optional)
grape tomatoes, cut in half

Directions

Cook pasta and in the last 5 minutes add the broccoli florets and cook for an additional 5 minutes or until broccoli and pasta are tender. Drain and rinse with cold water.

In a bowl, combine broccoli, pasta, parmesan and 1/8 tsp. each salt and ground pepper. Add oil and tomatoes and toss to combine well. Squeeze a lemon wedge over the salad before packing.

Salmon Salad

When you have leftover salmon for dinner, this is a great salad to have for lunch.

Ingredients
2 cooked Salmon Fillets
1 tbsp. fresh lemon juice
1 tbsp. whole-grain mustard
2 tbsp. red onion, finely chopped
4 tsp. mayonnaise

Directions
Stir together chopped salmon, red onion, lemon juice, mayonnaise, and mustard and pack in lunch boxes. Add in crackers or bread to go with the salad.

Pepperoni Salad

Ingredients
1 (8 oz.) pkg. lettuce greens
4 Cup cherry tomatoes
1/2 sweet red onion, diced
1/2 red pepper, diced
1 (6 oz.) pkg. sliced pepperoni
1/4 Cup mozzarella cheese, shredded
1/2 Cup extra virgin olive oil
1/3 Cup white balsamic vinegar
1 tsp parsley
1/8 tsp dried basil
1 garlic clove, minced
salt and pepper to taste
1 (5.5 oz.) box Italian seasoned croutons

Directions
In lunch containers, layer lettuce, tomatoes, onion, pepper, pepperoni and cheese. In a jar with a tight-fitting lid place the olive oil and vinegar. Add in the parsley, basil, garlic, salt and pepper. Tighten the lid and shake until all the ingredients are combined well. Add salad dressing in a small container and pack with the lunch box to go with the salad. Add a side of croutons to the lunch box.

Fruit and Nutty Salmon Salad

Ingredients
handful of salad leaves
1/3-1/2 Cup cooked salmon, broken up
2 Tablespoons cashew nuts
5-6 cherry tomatoes
sprinkle of pomegranate seeds, Craisins or raisins

Method
Combine all the ingredients in a lunch container and blend together.
Season with salt and pepper to taste ad pack for kids.
~Add whichever nuts your kids like and/or substitute pomegranate seeds with other dried fruit.

Ranch Chicken and Pepper Salad
Ingredients
1 (10 oz) pkg. of mixed greens, torn
1 (6 oz.) pkg. cooked chicken breast strips
1/2 Cup red, orange and yellow sweet pepper strips
1/2 Cup cherry tomatoes
1/4 Cup red onion, sliced, optional
1/2 Cup creamy Ranch dressing

Directions
In a salad bowl, add mixed greens, pepper strips, tomatoes, red onion and chicken strips. Place in lunch containers and add a side of salad dressing.
Makes 4 servings

SANDWICHES

Cold Cut sandwich

Ingredients
2 submarine rolls or sandwich bread
1 Tablespoon ranch dressing, mayonnaise or Italian salad dressing
4 ounces provolone cheese, thinly sliced
4 ounces salami, thinly sliced
4 ounces ham, thinly sliced
thin slice roasted chicken
2 red bell peppers, sliced into strips
1/2 head shredded iceberg lettuce
1 medium tomato, sliced

Directions
Cut open each roll and spread ranch dressing, mayonnaise or Italian salad dressing, which ever you like on the insides of the rolls.
Layer cheese and meats into the sandwich and finish with lettuce, tomato slices and peppers. Wrap up for packed lunches.
~Other suggestions for veggies to add could be shredded carrots, chopped cucumbers, or olive slices.

Italian Au Jus French Sandwich

Ingredients
1 (18.5 oz.) can of French onion soup
1/2 tsp dried Italian seasoning
3/4 lb. roast beef, sliced thin
6 (3 to 4 in) French rolls
6 slices of provolone cheese

Directions
In a microwave safe bowl, add soup and Italian seasoning. Warm for 2 minutes. Add in roast beef slices. Place several slices of roast beef and cheese in a lunch container. In the lunchbox, add a French roll cut in half in a plastic sandwich bag, roast beef container and a side of au jus for dipping.
At lunchtime kids can put their sandwich together.

Makes 6 sandwiches

Biscuit Sticks

These are like a sandwich rolled up all in one.

Ingredients
2 Cups flour
2 teaspoons Sugar
1/4 teaspoon salt
2/3 Cup milk
3 teaspoons Baking powder
1/2 teaspoon Cream of tartar
1/2 cup shortening
1 cup Chopped ham
1 Cup shredded cheese.

Directions
In mixer blend flour, sugar, salt, baking powder and cream of tartar. Add shortening and blend. Stir in milk until dough forms a ball. Stir in ham and cheese. Roll or pat dough into a rectangle. Cut into rectangle sticks and bake at 450 degrees for 10 minutes or until golden.

Pineapple Cream Cheese Sandwich

Ingredients

1 (8 oz.) pkg. cream cheese, softened
4 tbsp of crushed pineapple, drained well
4 bagels, bread slices or other sliced bread
4 pineapple rings

Directions

Place the cream cheese into a mixing bowl.
Add the crushed pineapple and stir until smooth.
Spread the cream cheese mixture over the bottom half of the bagel.
Place a pineapple ring onto each bagel half.
Top with the remaining bagel half.

Makes 4 sandwiches

Pizza Dog Boat Bites

Ingredients
8 all beef hot dogs or sausages
2 (8 oz.) cans of pizza sauce
8 hot dog buns
1 C of pizza cheese blend, shredded

Directions
Cut the hot dogs into strips. Place the cut hot dogs into a saucepan.
Pour the pizza sauce over the hot dogs, stirring gently to coat.
Place the pan over medium heat and cook 5 minutes or until hot, stirring often. Open the hot dog buns. Spoon the hot dog mixture evenly into each bun. Sprinkle each boat evenly with the cheese. Close the buns and cut each bun into 4 equal size pieces.
Place several bites into a lunch container.
Makes 32 boat bites in all.

Classic Egg Salad

Sometimes, nothing is better than the taste of a classic homemade egg salad sandwich. This version of egg salad has all the traditional ingredients: mayo, celery, hard-boiled eggs, and mustard.

Ingredients

8 hard-cooked eggs, peeled and chopped
2 tbsp. celery, chopped, if your kids like
1/2 Cup mayonnaise
2 tsp. yellow mustard
Lettuce. chopped
Salt and pepper
Bread or crackers, to serve

Directions

Chop boiled eggs in a bowl. Stir in mustard, celery, and mayonnaise.
 Season with salt and pepper, to taste and stir gently to mix well.
Layer a lunch container with chopped lettuce and top with egg salad. Pack in bread on the side or crackers to put together during lunch time.
~Don't forget an ice pack in the lunch!
~If your kids don't like celery, leave it out and try using celery salt in place of plain salt.

Pear and Cheese Sandwiches

Ingredients
4 English muffins split in half
2 Tablespoons mustard, optional
4 Canadian bacon slices or ham slices
1 pear, peeled and sliced thin
4 slices of cheddar cheese

Directions
Spread the cut side of the English muffins with the mustard.
Place a slice of bacon on to 4 slices of muffin.
Lay a couple of the pear slices over the bacon.
Top each with a slice of cheese.
Cover each sandwich with the second slice of muffin.
Heat a large griddle or skillet over medium high heat.
Lay the sandwiches into the heated pan then adjust the heat to medium low.
Cook for 5 minutes then turn.
Cook for minutes longer or until browned and cheese starts to melt. Allow to cool slightly and wrap in waxed paper or lunch container
Makes 4 sandwiches

Pizza Quesadillas

Ingredients
8 flour tortillas
1 Cup pizza sauce
pepperoni slices
1 Cup mozzarella or cheddar cheese, shredded

How to Make It:
Warm up skillet or frying pan. Lay 4 tortillas out and spread with sauce. Top with shredded cheese and pepperoni. Top with another tortilla. Fry on both sides until golden brown. Cut into triangles. Place in lunch container.

You can leave the top off for an open pizza, if you'd like.

Fish Stick Burgers

Ingredients
9 frozen fish sticks
1/2 Cup or less mayonnaise
1 tsp taco seasoning
3 hamburger buns or hoagie rolls
1 tomato, sliced
3 lettuce leaves

Directions
Cook the fish sticks as directed on the box.
Place the mayonnaise into a small bowl and blend in taco seasoning mix.
Cut the buns open and spread the mayonnaise mixture over the inside. Add a lettuce leaf, 3 fish sticks, and top with a tomato slice. Wrap up for lunch.

Makes 3 sandwiches

Chicken Salad Sandwiches

Ingredients
2 cups rotisserie chicken, skin removed, chopped
1/2 cup mayonnaise with olive oil
1/3 cup carrot, shredded
Pinch of paprika
1 clove garlic, minced
2 Tablespoons yellow mustard
Freshly ground pepper
1 tsp. celery salt
6 whole-wheat sourdough rolls
tomato, sliced
Lettuce, chopped

Directions
Add chopped chicken, mayonnaise, carrot, mustard, paprika, celery salt and a dash of ground pepper. Mix to combine well.
Pack the chicken salad in a lunch container and add a roll, tomato and lettuce.

Fruited Bagel Spread

Ingredients
1/2 Cup of strawberry cream cheese, softened
1 large red apple, cored and chopped small
1-2 strawberries, chopped small
2 bananas, chopped small
4 cinnamon flavored or plain bagels

Directions
Place the cream cheese in a bowl and stir until smooth and creamy.
Fold in the apples and bananas until well coated.
Divide spreads into small containers.
Cut the bagels in half and toast each half in the toaster until slightly crispy.
Allow to cool slightly and place in a lunch container.
Pack a small container of fruity spread to go with the toasted bagel pieces.
~You don't need to toast bagel if you'd rather not. Just add to sandwich baggie as is.

Bacon Double Grilled Cheese

Ingredients
2 teaspoons butter
2 pieces of Texas toast
1 slice of Cheddar cheese
3 slices bacon, cooked crisp
2 slices of sweet red bell pepper
1 slice of Swiss cheese
Lettuce leaf

Directions
Cook bacon until crisp and place on a paper towel to drain. Spread the butter on one side of each piece of Texas toast. Add toast to a hot skillet butter side down. Layer with a slice of Cheddar cheese, bacon, bell pepper slices, lettuce leaf and a slice of Swiss cheese.
Place the second piece of Texas toast, butter side up on the top. Grill for 3 minutes. Turn and continue grilling an additional 3 minutes or until browned and the cheese has begun to melt.

Makes 1 serving

Make Ahead Subs

Ingredients
1 (16 oz) loaf of French bread
1/2 Cup sour cream ranch dip
3/4 Cup pkg. shredded carrots
1 Cup lettuce, shredded
1/2 of a cucumber, peeled, seeded and shredded
2 oz thin sliced deli roast beef
2 oz. thin sliced deli ham
2 oz. thin sliced deli turkey
2 oz thin sliced deli chicken
4 oz thin sliced provolone cheese

Directions
Cut the bread loaf in half lengthwise.
Spread the sour cream ranch dip onto the cut sides of the bread.
Layer the carrots, lettuce, cucumbers, all 4 types of meat and the cheese onto one side of the cut bread.
Close the bread over the top.
Wrap tightly in saran wrap and refrigerate for up to 8 hours.
To serve, cut into 8 slices and place in a lunch baggie or wrap in plastic wrap.
Makes 8 servings

Turkey Burger Pita Wraps

Ingredients
1/2 Cup mayonnaise
2 tsp curry powder
1 lb. ground turkey breast
2 oz feta cheese with basil and tomato, crumbled
1/2 tsp salt
4 pita flat bread
8 red onion slices
8 Romaine or spinach leaves

Directions
Set the broiler to preheat. Place the mayonnaise into a small mixing bowl. Add the curry powder and mix until blended together well. Place the ground turkey into a large mixing bowl. Add 2 T of the mayonnaise mixture. Sprinkle in the feta cheese. Add the salt and mix until all the ingredients are well combined. Make into 4 patties. Place the patties on the rack of a broiler pan. Broil 4 inches from the heat for 12 minutes being sure to turn the burger half way through the cooking time. Spread the remaining mayonnaise mixture onto the pita bread slices. Place a patty onto one side of the pita bread.
Add 2 slices of onion and 2 spinach leaves on top of the burger.
Fold the pita over the top of the burger.

BTST Sandwich

Ingredients
1/4 Cup salad dressing
8 slices bread, toasted
12 slices bacon, cooked crisp and drained well
8 thin slices of deli turkey
2 tomatoes, sliced
8 fresh spinach leaves

Directions
Spread the salad dressing on one side of each slice of toasted bread.
Lay 3 slices of bacon onto each of 4 slices of bread.
Top the bacon with 2 slices of ham.
Add 2 slices of tomato to each sandwich and top with 2 spinach leaves.
Place the other slices of bread, salad dressing down onto the top of each sandwich.

Makes 4 servings

Club Salad Pitas

Ingredients
mixed salad greens
chopped tomatoes
deli meat; ham, turkey or chicken, whichever you like
rotisserie chicken
Sliced cheese
Ranch salad dressing or mayonnaise
hard boiled eggs, sliced
pita bread
other toppings could include: chopped olives, chopped pickles

Directions
Using Ranch dressing or mayonnaise, spread inside of pita bread. Add desired chef salad toppings, whatever your favorite toppings are.

More Main Dishes

Peanut Satay Chicken Drumsticks

Ingredients
6 chicken thighs or drumsticks
1/2 tsp pepper
1/3 Cup creamy peanut butter
2 Tablespoons soy sauce
3 Tablespoons orange juice

Directions
Season the chicken thighs with the pepper on both sides. Place the chicken in the crock pot. In a large mixing bowl, stir together the peanut butter, soy sauce and orange juice. Pour over the chicken. Cook covered 4-6 hours or until chicken is tender. Allow to cool before adding to lunchbox container.

Fruity Oatmeal in a Thermos

Ingredients
1/4 Cup steel cut oats
1 1/2 Cup boiling water
1/4 Cup dried fruit (your favorite)

Directions
Add oats to a thermos. Pour boiling water into the thermos. Screw lid on and let sit overnight. In the morning drain off any excess water. Stir in the dried fruit and place in your kids lunchbox. Great as a main dish or snack.
~Don't use instant oats in this recipe steel cut, old fashioned oats or quick oats work best.

Rice Balls

Directions

With 3 Cups rice, we made 13 medium size rice balls. Hot rice is easiest to mold so once it is done cooking work quickly forming your balls.

Cook your rice. While it is cooking get the following items ready.

Muffin scoop
Small bowl or cup
Fillings
Plastic wrap
Salt

I've found the best method for making this is the following. Layer a sheet of plastic wrap over your small bowl. When your rice is done cooking, use your muffin scoop and fill the bowl half full. Sprinkle with salt. Push your fillings inside the middle. Wrap your plastic wrap around your ball and squeeze together. Unwrap and place on a serving plate. Continue until your rice is done. Serve. If you'd like to save some for the next day's lunch wrap the balls in plastic wrap again and store in refrigerator.

Filling Suggestions

Our favorite rice balls fillings are:
Plain Rice balls with mini meatballs kebob on the side
Rice balls filled with marble size cooked teriyaki meatballs inside
Rice balls with cooked teriyaki chicken or pork cube inside
Cook a roast chicken, cool and shred. Sprinkle chicken with soy sauce and ginger. Add to rice balls according to directions below.

SNACKS & TREATS

Pumpkin Seed Trail Mix

Ingredients

4 cups flakes cereal, such as Frosted Flakes, Raisin Bran Flakes or Cornflakes
1 cup pumpkin seeds
2 cups small pretzel twists
1/4 cup miniature semisweet chocolate baking bits, such as M&M's mini
1cup dried apricots, chopped
1/2 Cup dried Craisins
1/2 Cup almonds

Directions

In a large bowl, combine all the ingredients together. Store in sealed plastic container.

Frozen Strawbana Smoothies

This recipe makes enough to freeze several small containers for more than one packed lunch.

Ingredients

3 bananas cut in pieces
16 oz.pkg frozen strawberries
1-1/4 cup 100%orange juice or pineapple juice
1 Cup vanilla or plain yogurt
2 tbsp. ground flaxseed

Directions

Combine all the ingredients in a blender and blend until smooth. Pour smoothie into small plastic containers with secure lids. Freeze at least overnight. When ready to pack, take out of freezer and add to lunch box. By lunchtime, it will soften up.

Strawberry Oatmeal Bars

These sweet strawberry-oatmeal bars are sure to become a lunchbox favorite that even the pickiest eaters will love.

Ingredients

1 1/2 cup oats
1 1/2 cups flour
1 cup unsalted butter, cubed, and some more for coating the pan
1 tsp. baking powder
1 Cup strawberry jam
1/2 cup brown sugar
1/2 tsp. salt

Directions

Preheat your oven to 350°F. Coat a 9×13-inch pan with cooking spray or butter.
In a bowl, combine oats, flour, butter, baking powder, sugar, and salt.
Place half of the mixture into the coated pan and press down to make a crust.
Spread strawberry jam over all the crust.
Cover with the remaining oat mixture and press into jam.
Place the pan in the oven and bake for about 35-40 minutes. or until golden brown.
Let cool before cutting into squares. Store in sandwich baggies and freeze for lunch boxes.

Chewy Oatmeal Raisin Cookies

Ingredients

1/2 cup all-purpose flour
1 1/2 cups old-fashioned rolled oats
1 tsp. pure vanilla extract
1/2 cup raisins or Craisins
1 large egg
6 tbsp. unsalted butter, room temperature
1/2 tsp. baking soda
1/4 cup granulated sugar
1/2 cup packed dark-brown sugar
1/2 tsp. salt

Directions

Preheat oven to 350°F. In a mixer, cream together butter, white and brown sugar. Add in vanilla and egg and blend until well combined.
In separate bowl, stir together dry ingredients, including oats, flour, baking soda, raisins, and salt. Add dry ingredients into wet ingredients and mix until well combined. Drop by spoonfuls or muffin scoops onto cookie sheets. Bake for 12-15 minutes or until golden brown.
Let cool and store individually or by twos in sandwich baggies and freeze.

Apple-Cinnamon Granola

Ingredients
1 cup whole-grain toasted oat cereal
3 cups regular oats
1 cup dried apples, chopped
2 tbsp. brown sugar
1/4 cup honey
1/3 cup oat bran
1/3 cup applesauce
2 tbsp. butter
1/3 cup walnuts, finely chopped
2 tsp. ground cinnamon
Cooking spray

Directions
Preheat oven at 250 degrees F. In a large bowl, combine oats, oat cereal, oat bran, walnuts, and cinnamon; stir well to combine.
In microwave safe bowl, melt 2 tbsp. butter. Stir in honey, 1/3 cup applesauce, and brown sugar. Cook an additional 2 minutes.
Drizzle the honey mixture over the oat mixture and stir to coat well.
Evenly spread the mixture on a jelly-roll pan or cookie sheet.
Bake for about 1 hour, stirring every 30 minutes.
Let cool completely before stirring in the chopped apples. Store in an airtight container.
~Add any kind of dried fruit your family likes, we like diced dried apricots and Craisins.

PB Chocolate Rice Krispy Treats

Ingredients

3/4 cup peanut-butter chips
6 cups puffed rice cereal
4 tbsp. butter, sliced
8 ounces finely chopped semisweet chocolate
1 bag (10-ounces) small marshmallows

Directions

In a microwave safe dish, melt butter. Add in marshmallows and chocolate and cook in one-minute intervals, stirring after each minute, until melted. Remove from microwave with hot pad and gently stir in peanut butter chips and rice cereal.
Using cooking spray, grease a 9×13-inch baking pan. Using a wet or buttered spatula spread the mixture into the baking dish. Let set and cut into squares.

Homemade Pecan Sandies

Ingredients
1 cup pecans, coarsely chopped
1 cup all-purpose flour
1 1/2 tsp. pure vanilla extract
1/2 cup packed light-brown sugar
1/2 cup unsalted butter, at room temperature
1/4 tsp. salt

Directions
In a mixing bowl, cream together butter and sugar until fluffy. Add in vanilla and salt.
By hand stir in pecans. Using a small muffin scoop, scoop onto cookie sheets and flatten with hand or bottom of cup. Bake in a 350-degree preheated oven for 15-18 minutes or until golden brown. Let cool and store individually or by twos in sandwich baggies. Freeze extras for future lunches.

Oat Rice PB Balls

Ingredients

2 tbsp. unsalted butter
1 cup quick oats
1 1/2 cups Rice Krispies cereal
1 tsp. vanilla extract
3 tbsp. honey
1/4 cup powdered sugar
2/3 cup peanut butter, natural is the best choice
1/4 cup peanuts, chopped
1/4 cup mini chocolate chips
1/4 cup raisins

Directions

In a microwave safe dish, melt butter. Stir in vanilla, honey, sugar, and peanut butter.
Stir in the oats and Rice Krispies. Stir in chocolate chips and raisins. Blend until well combined. Roll into balls and then roll each ball in chopped peanuts. Place on cookie sheet and chill several hours. Add several balls to kids lunches and freeze extras in sandwich baggies.
Makes about 24 balls

Grape and Pecans in a Thermos
Ingredients
1 (4 oz) pkg. cream cheese at room temperature
1 (4 oz) container sour cream
1/4 Cup white vinegar
1/2 tsp vanilla extract
2 lbs seedless grapes
2 oz pecans, chopped, optional
1 tbsp brown sugar

Directions
Place the softened cream cheese in a large mixing bowl. Add the sour cream and stir to blend. Pour in the vinegar and the vanilla extract. Mix well being sure the mixture is smooth and creamy. Fold in the grapes carefully making sure all the grapes are covered well with the creamy mixture. Refrigerate until chilled about 30 minutes. Stir in the pecans and brown sugar. Place in a pre-chilled thermos.

Printed in Great Britain
by Amazon